My Heart, My Valentine & the Color of Love:

Adult Coloring Book

100% Original Coloring Pages

ADULT COLORING BOOKS SERIES

Mix Books, LLC

mix-booksonline.com

Be one of the In Crowd!

As a Mix Books Coloring Insider, you will receive FREE coloring pages to download and be among the first to know about special offers and our newest coloring books.
Sign up now, and as our thanks to you, immediately receive TEN illustrations in PDF format. Go to:

http://www.mix-booksonline.com/coloring

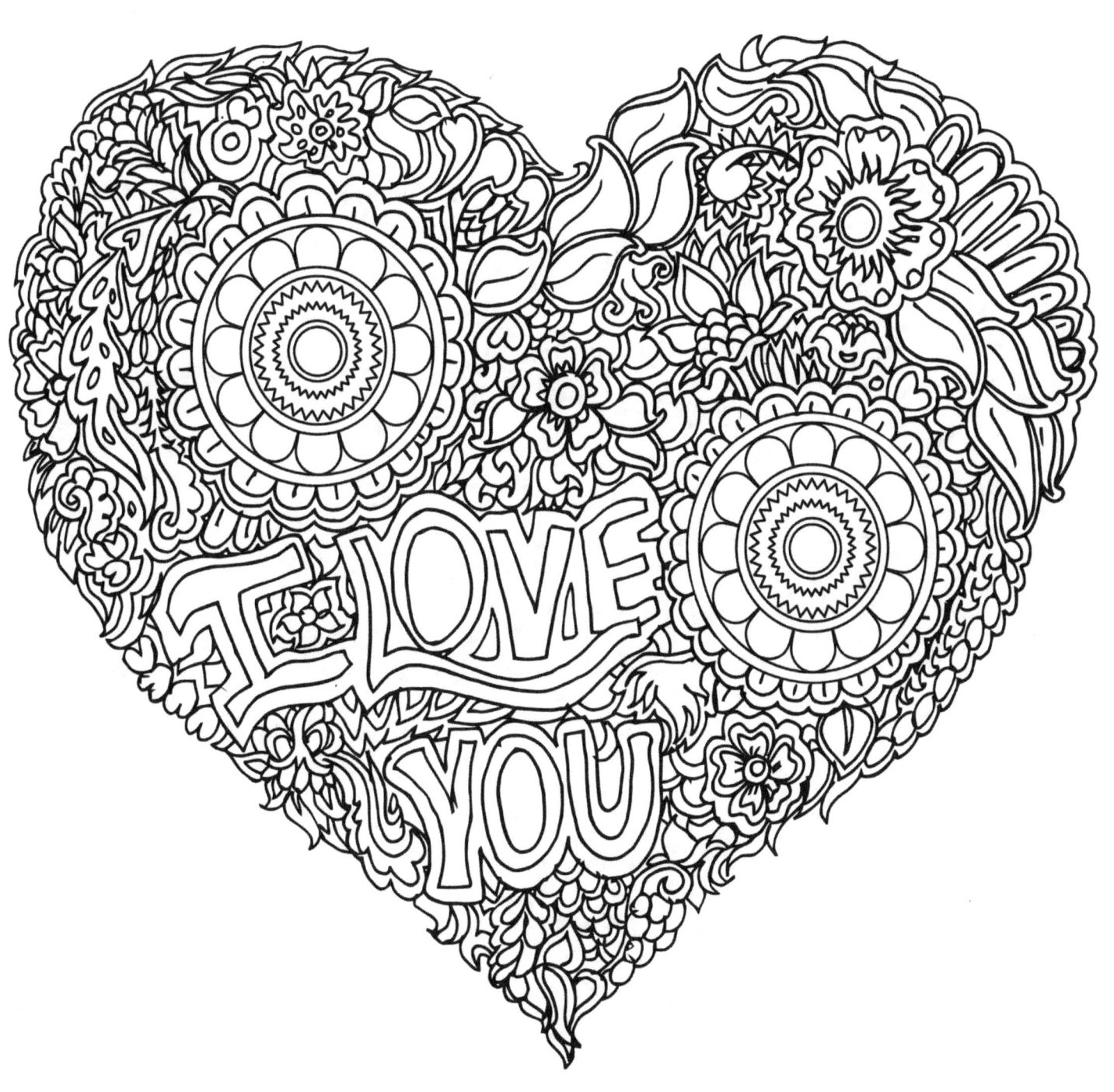

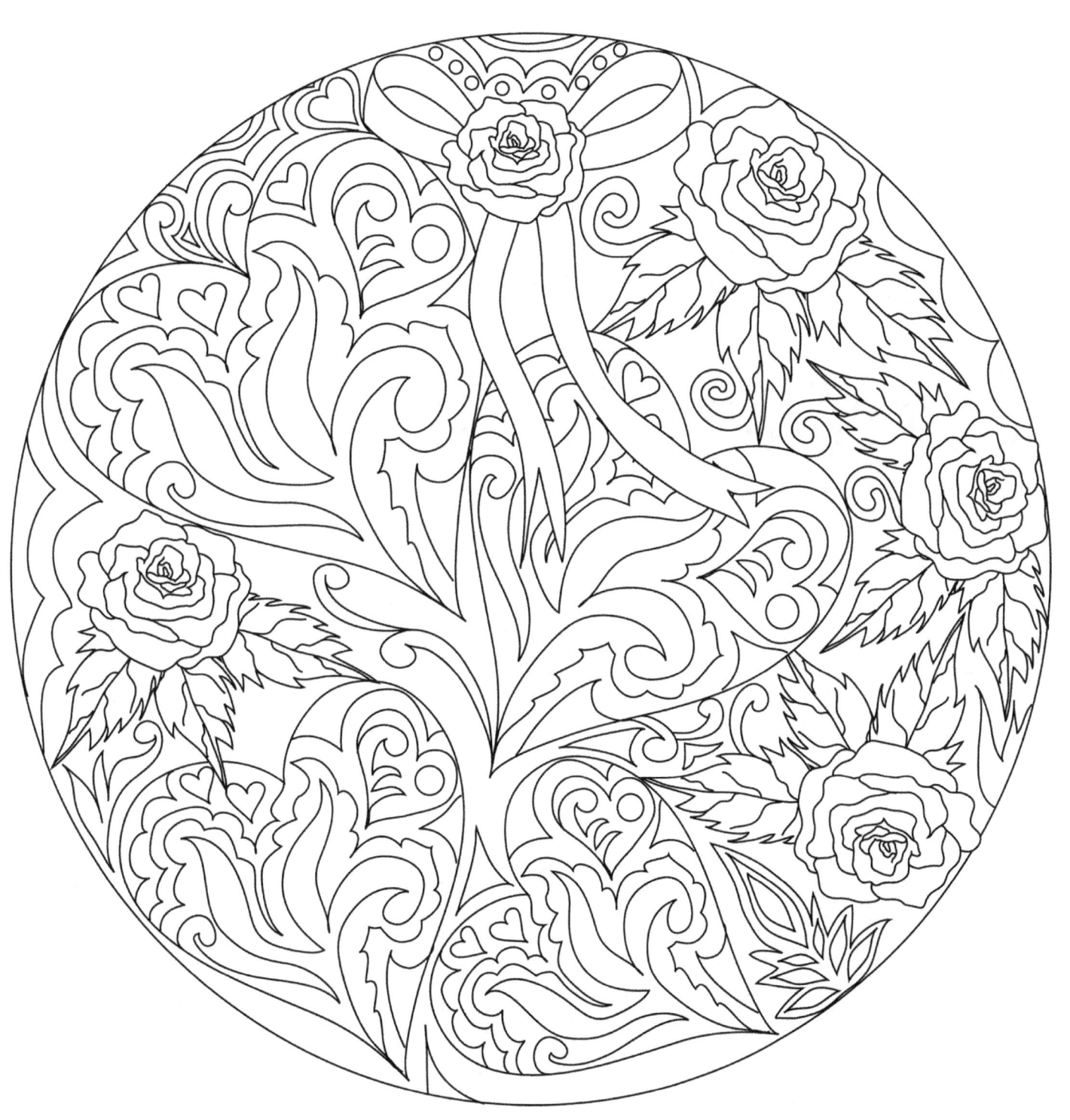

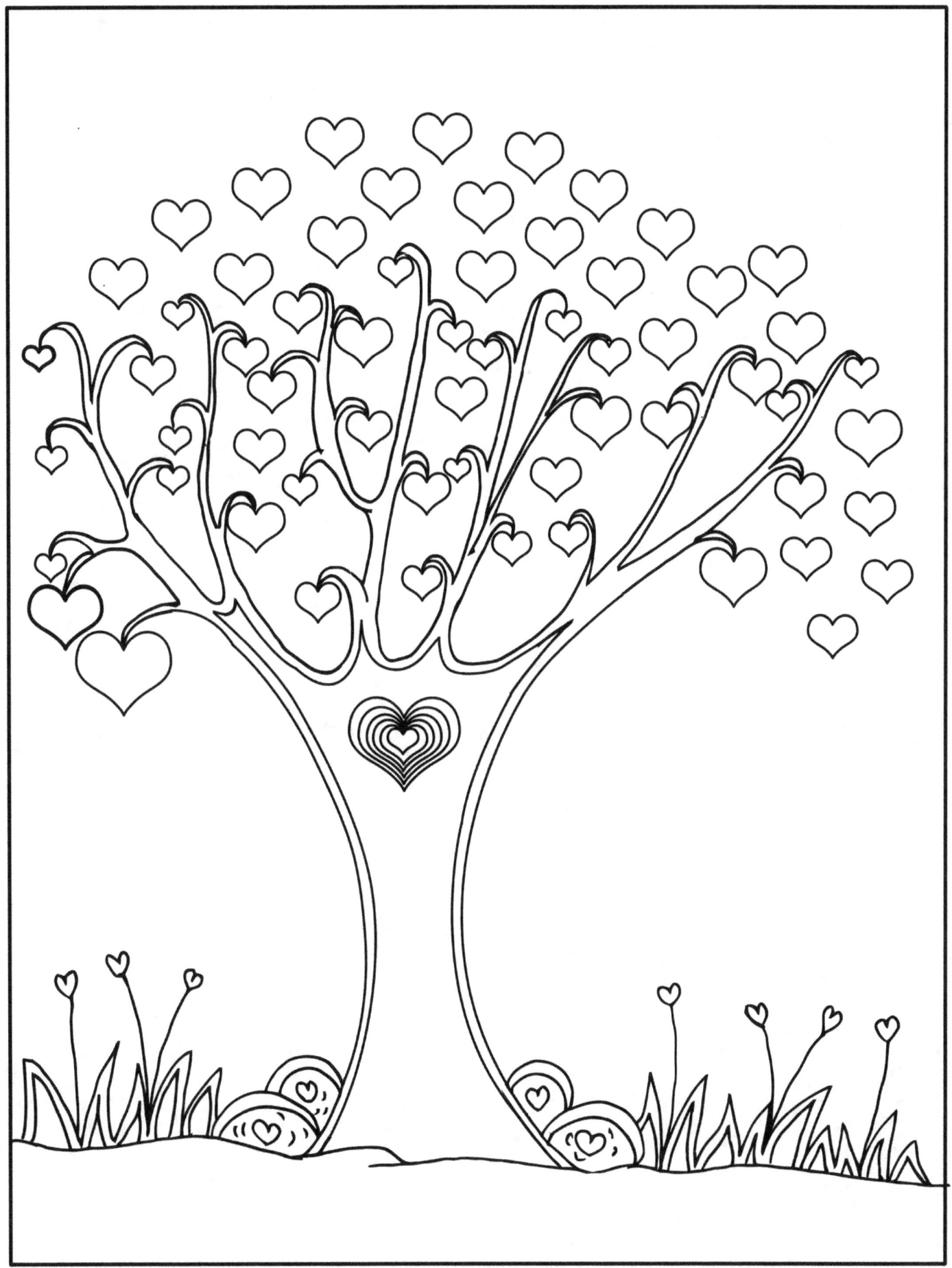

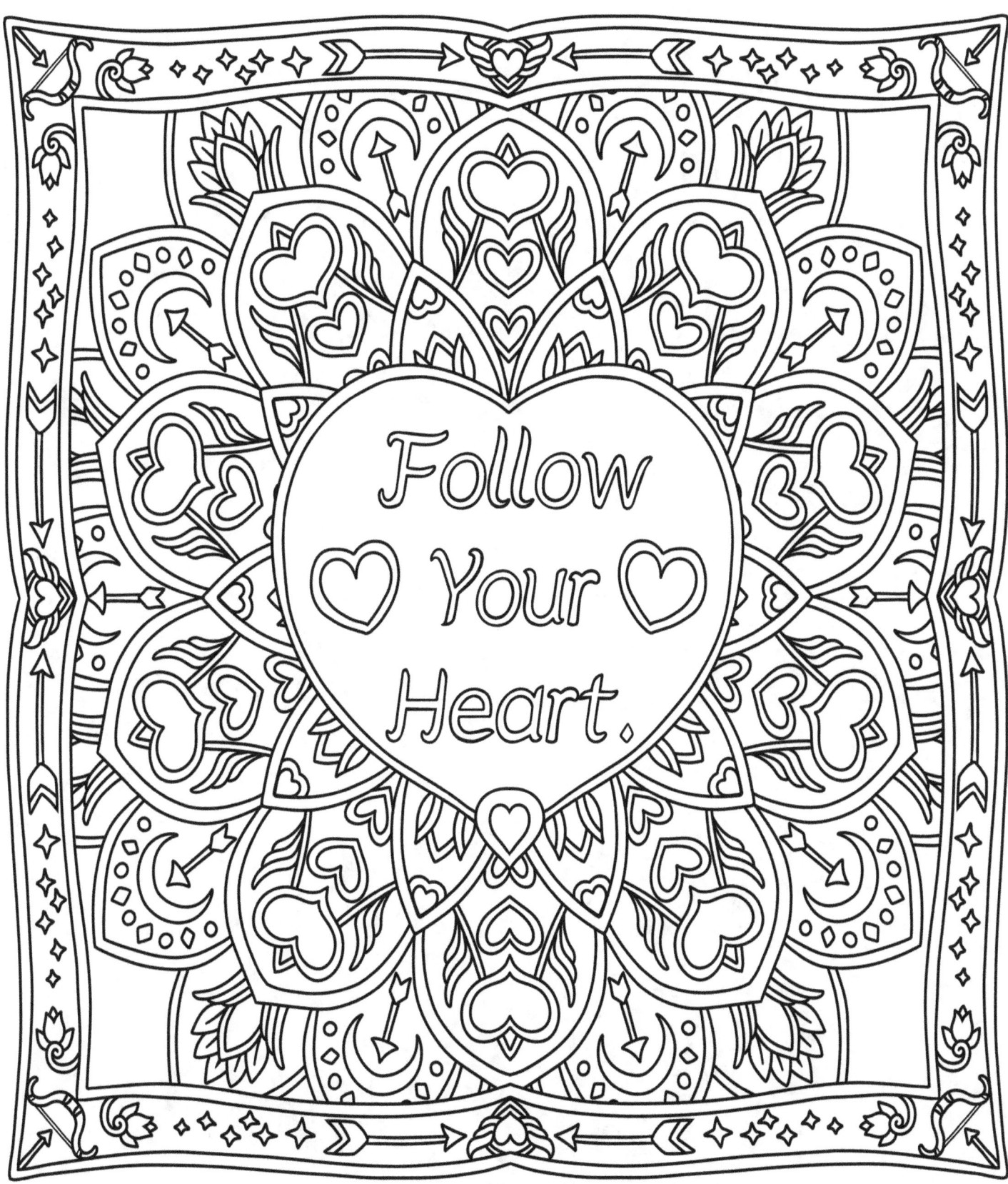

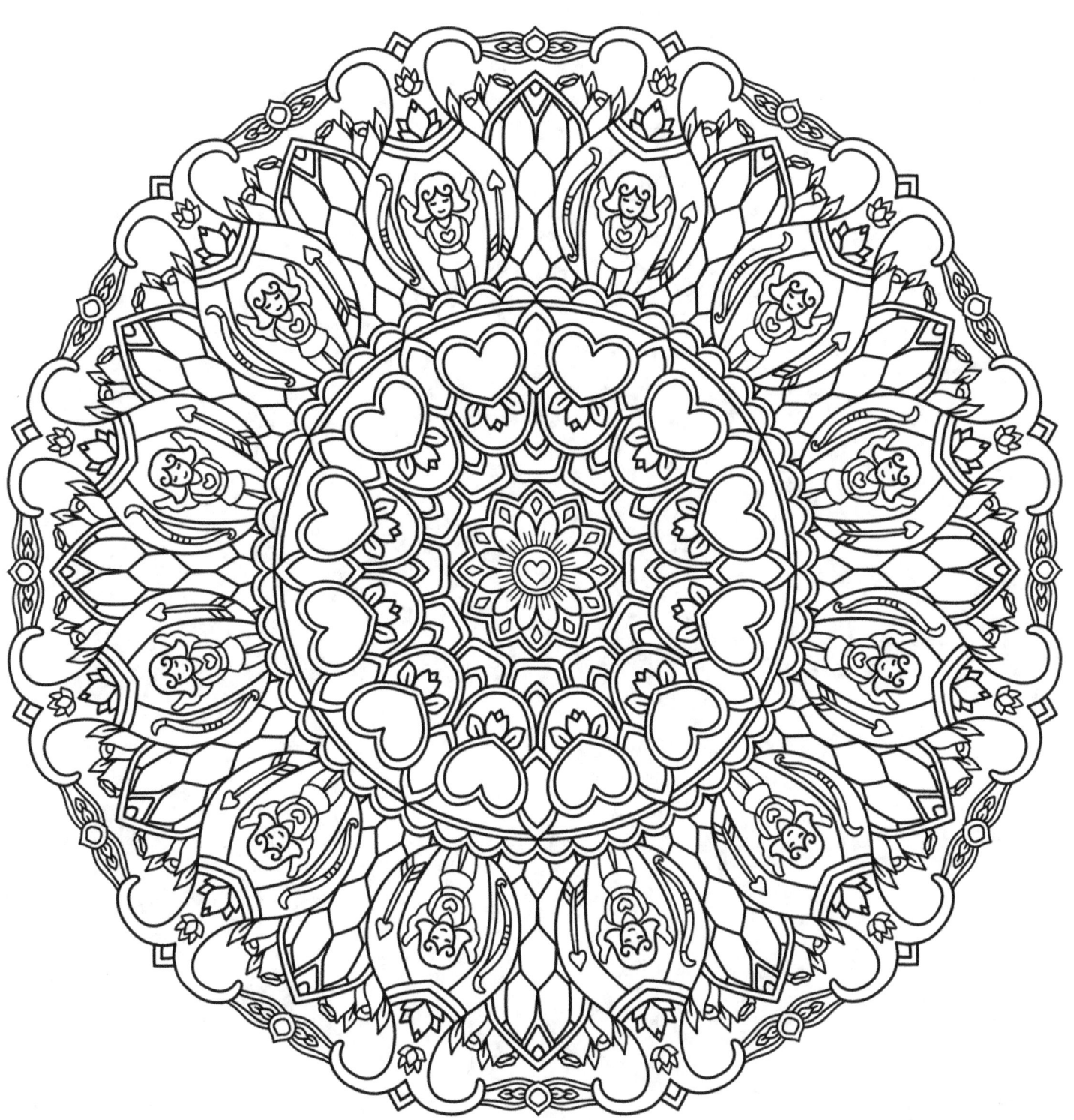

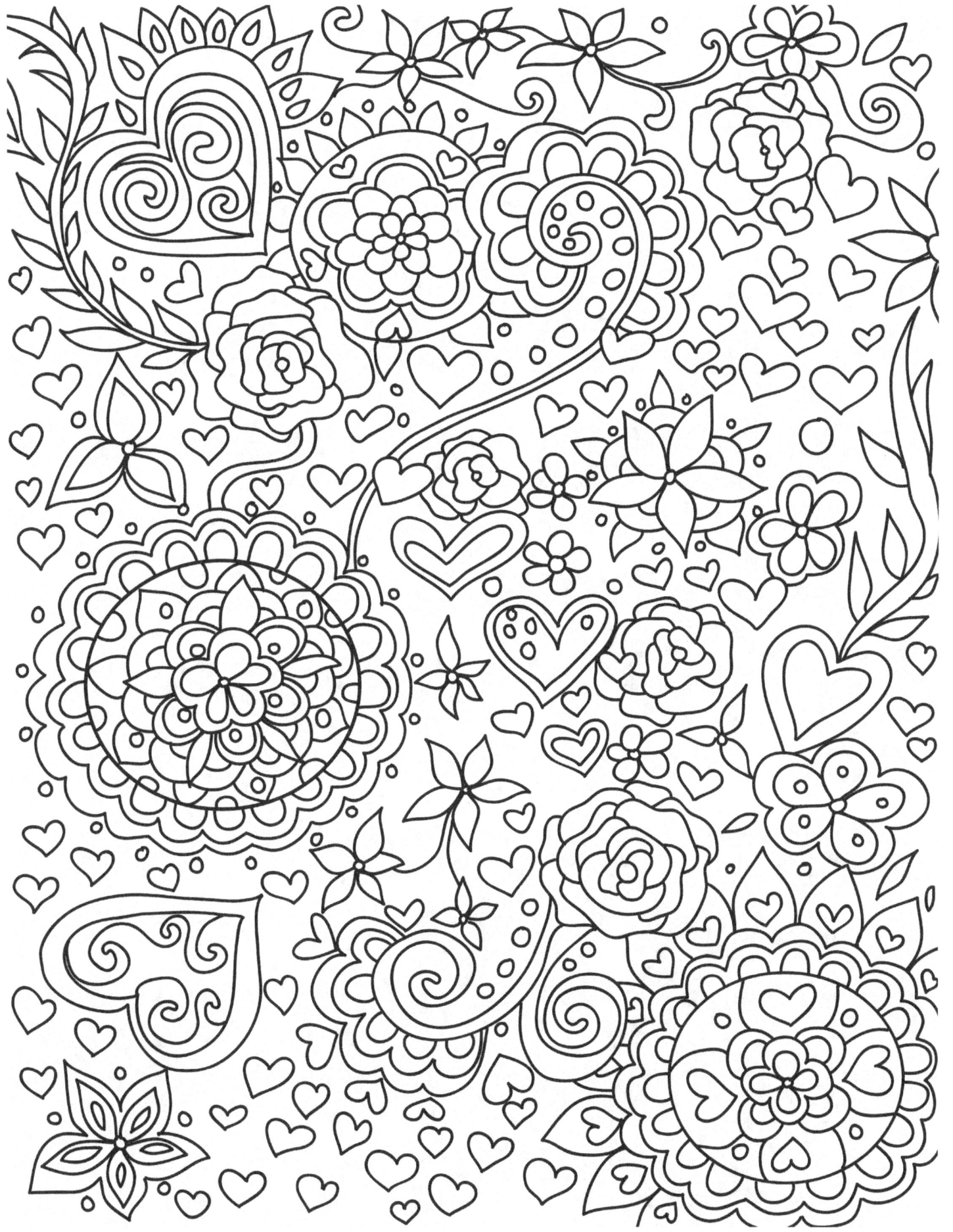

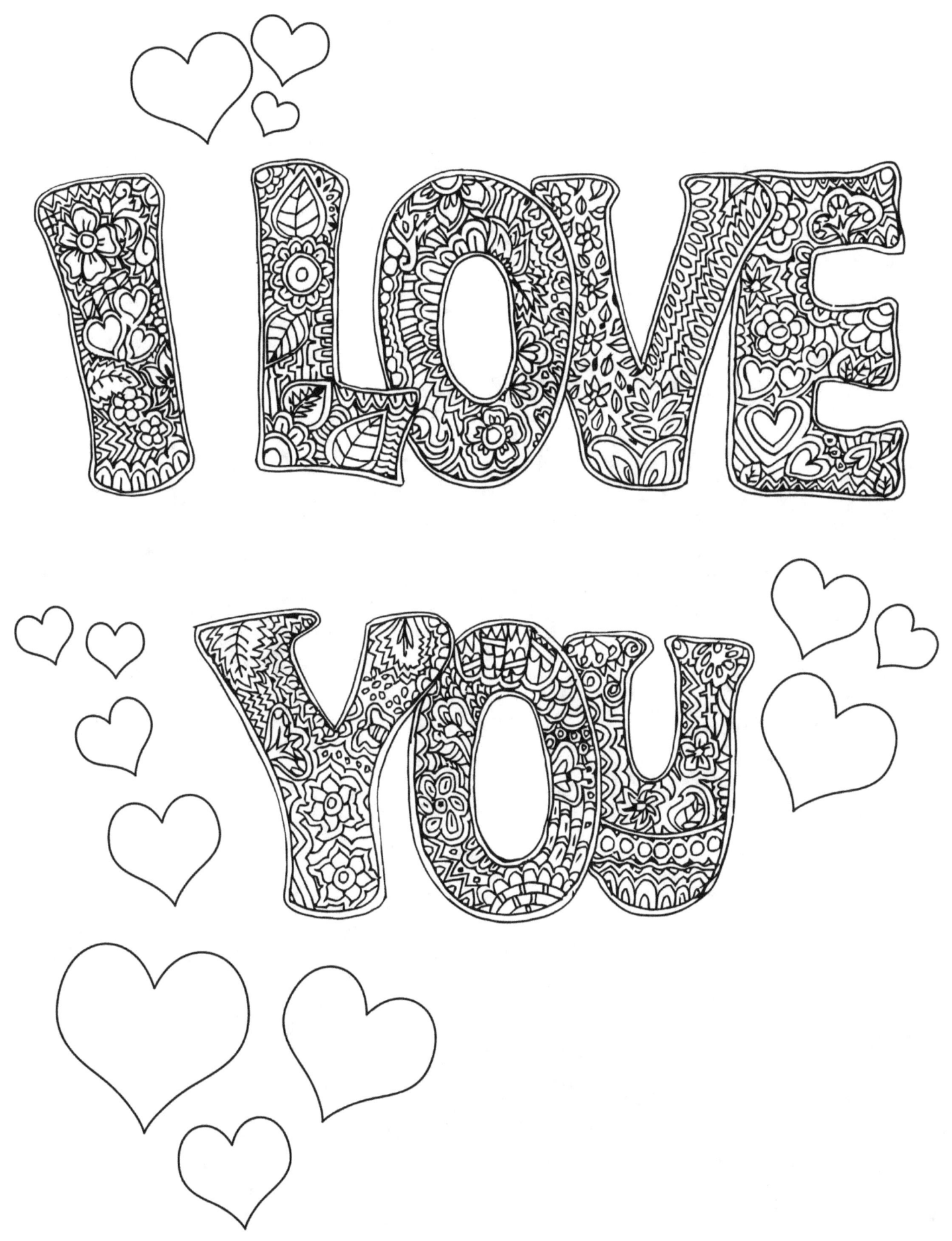

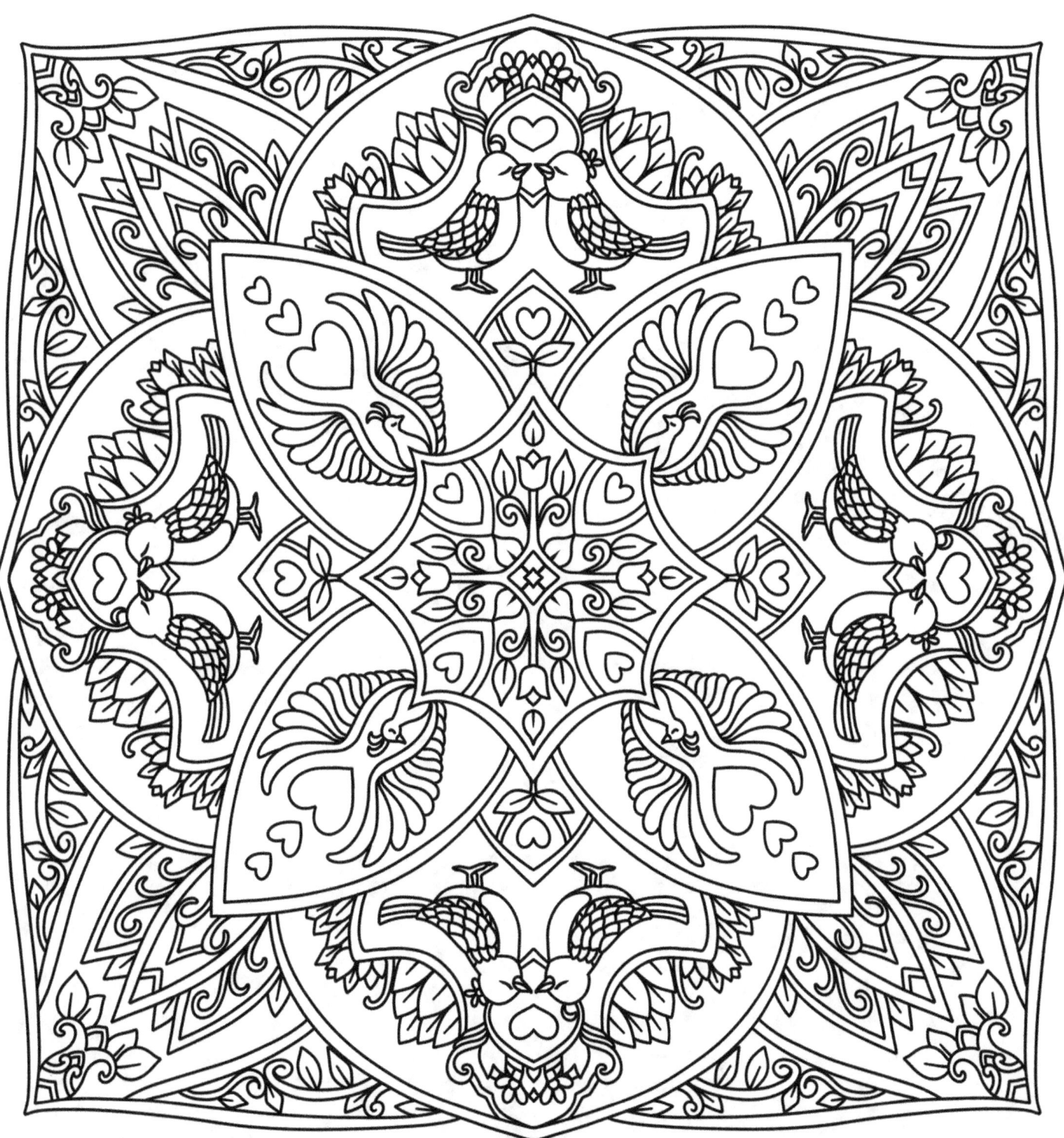

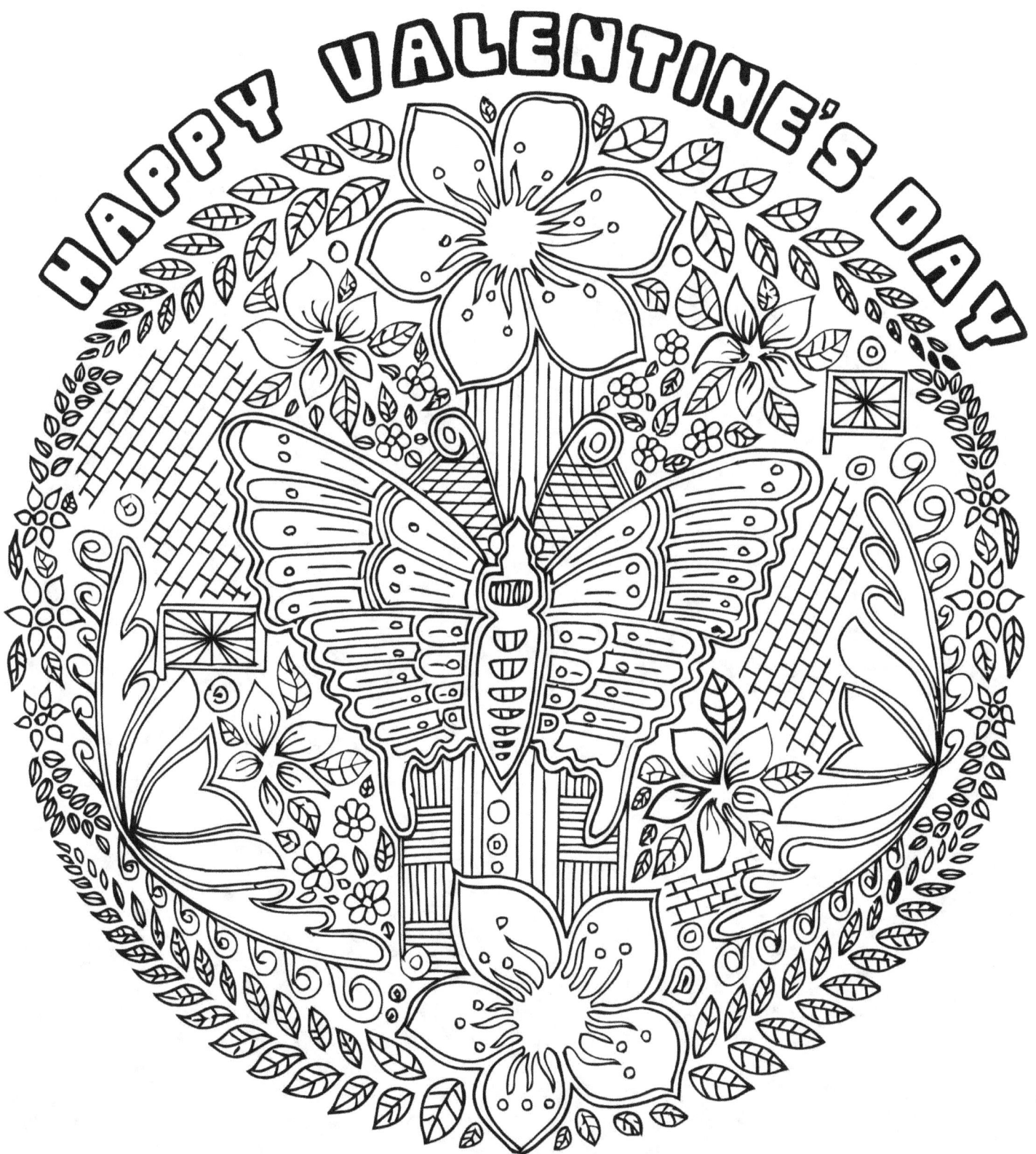

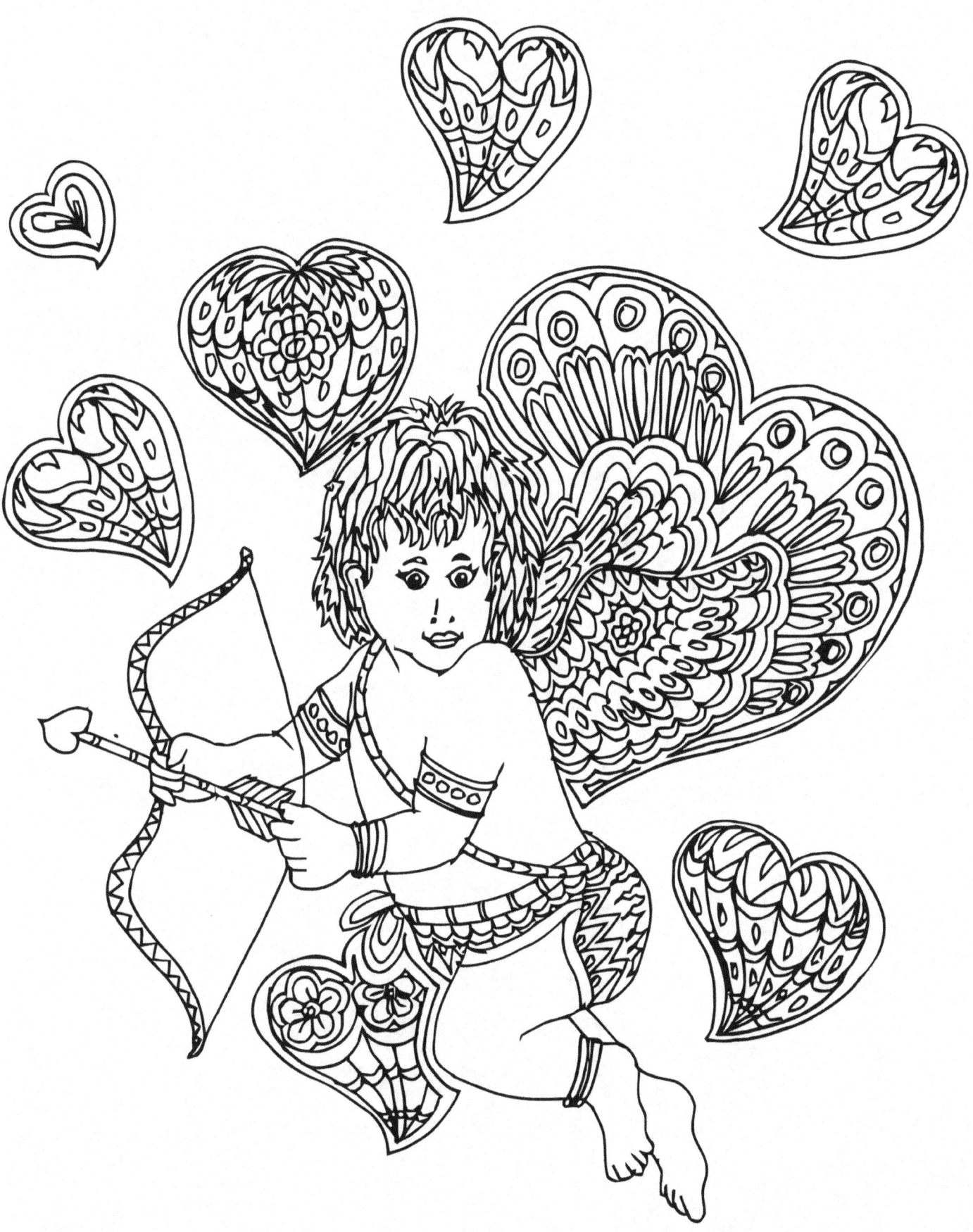

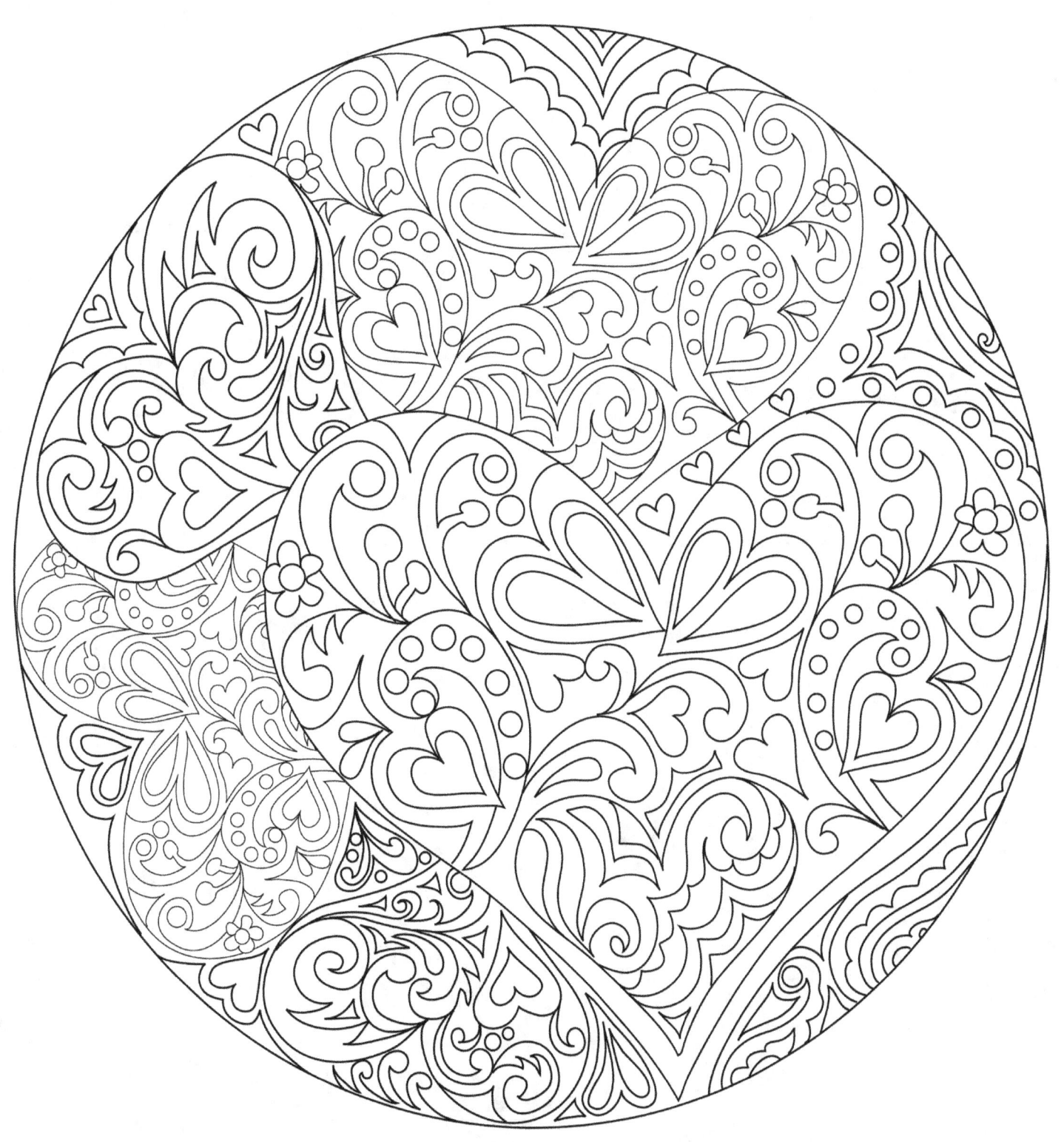

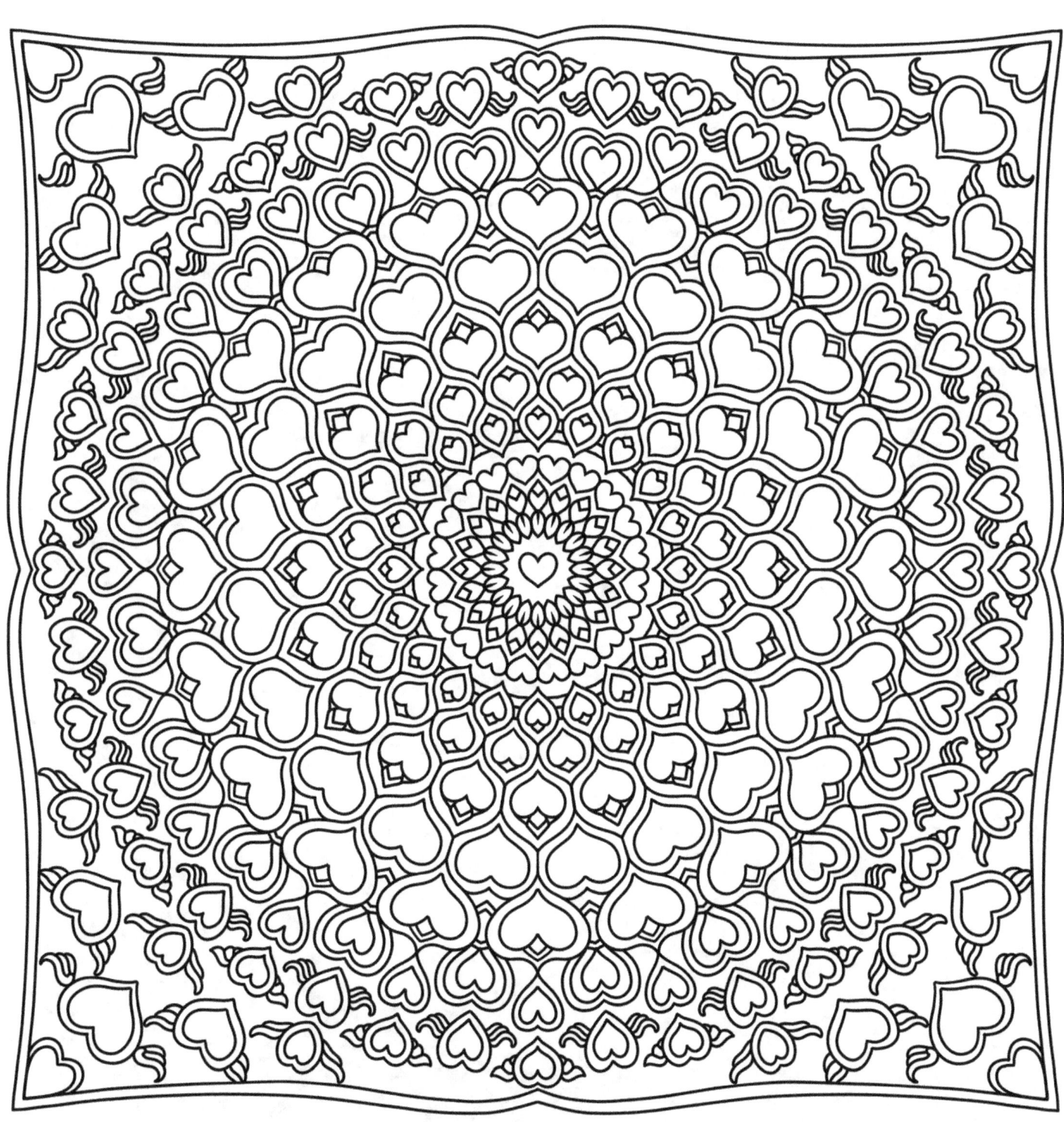

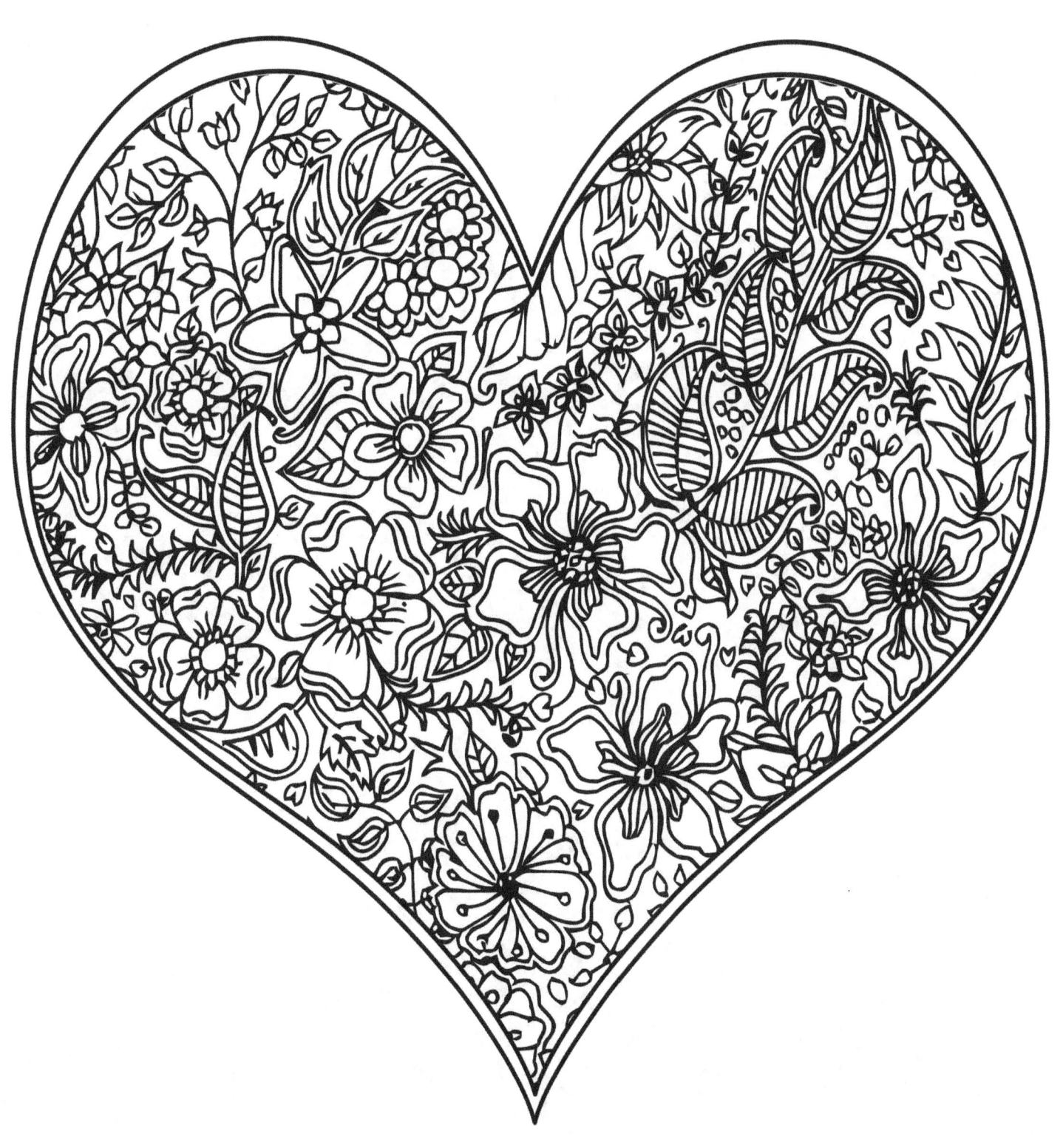

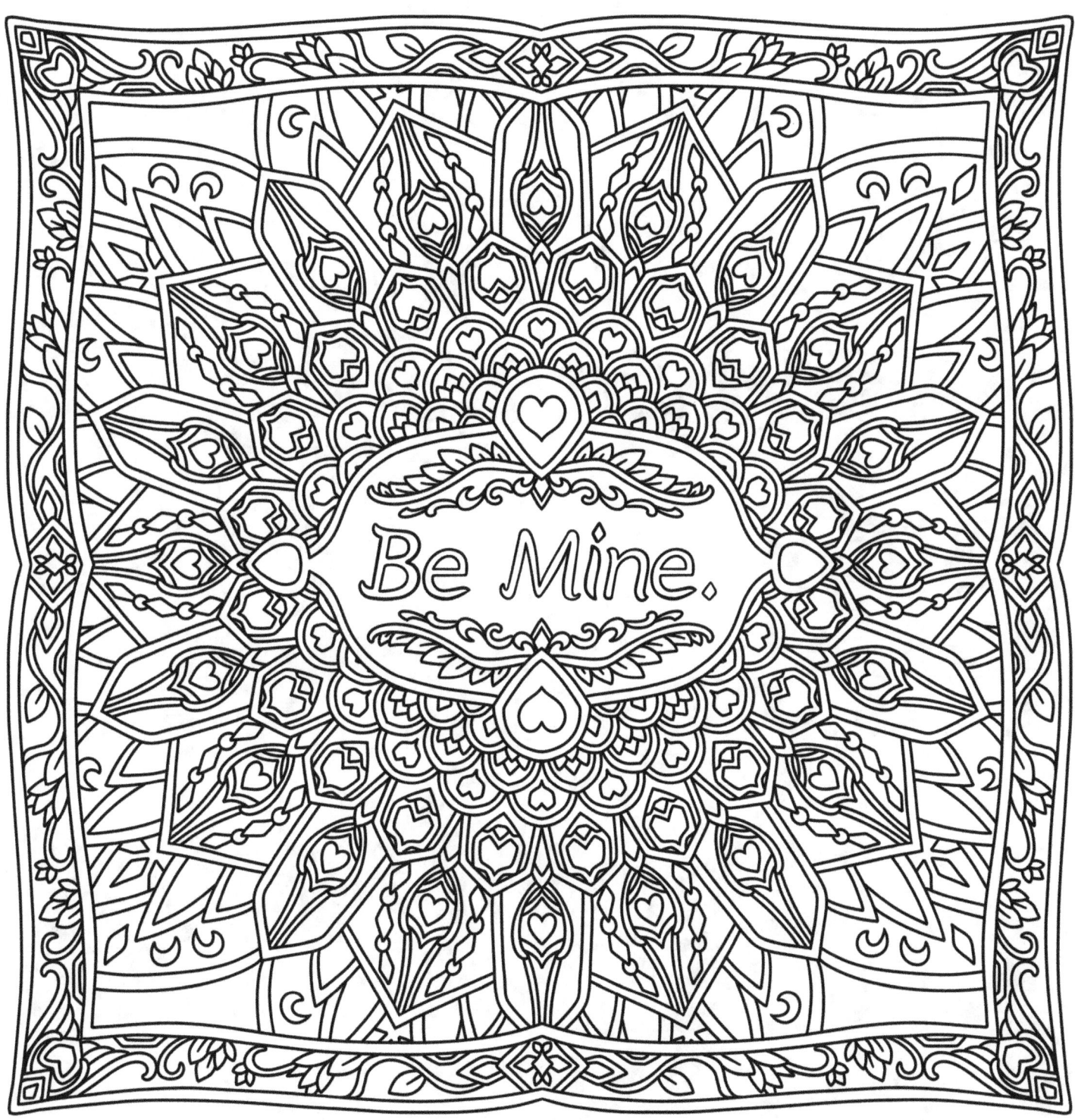

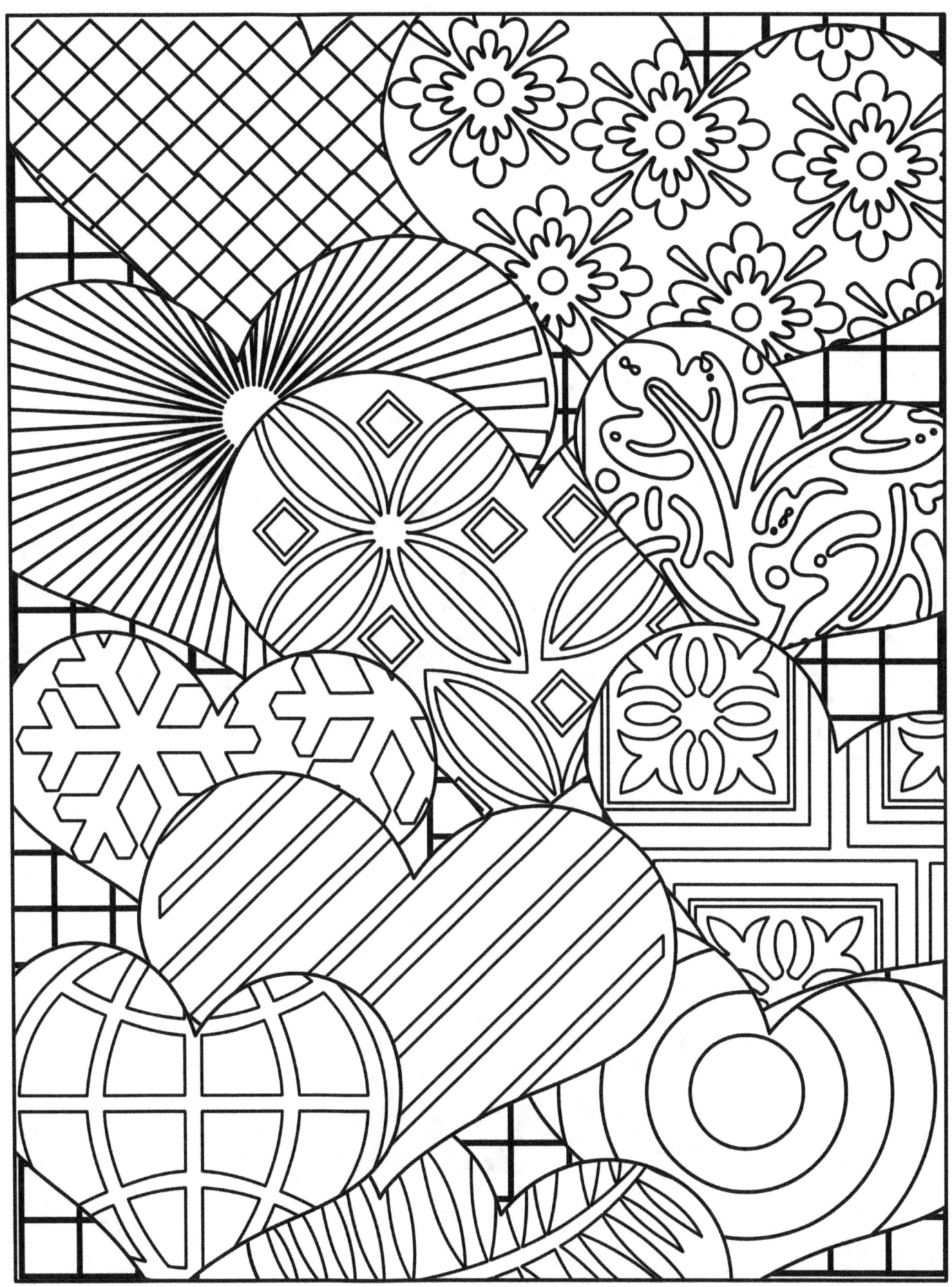

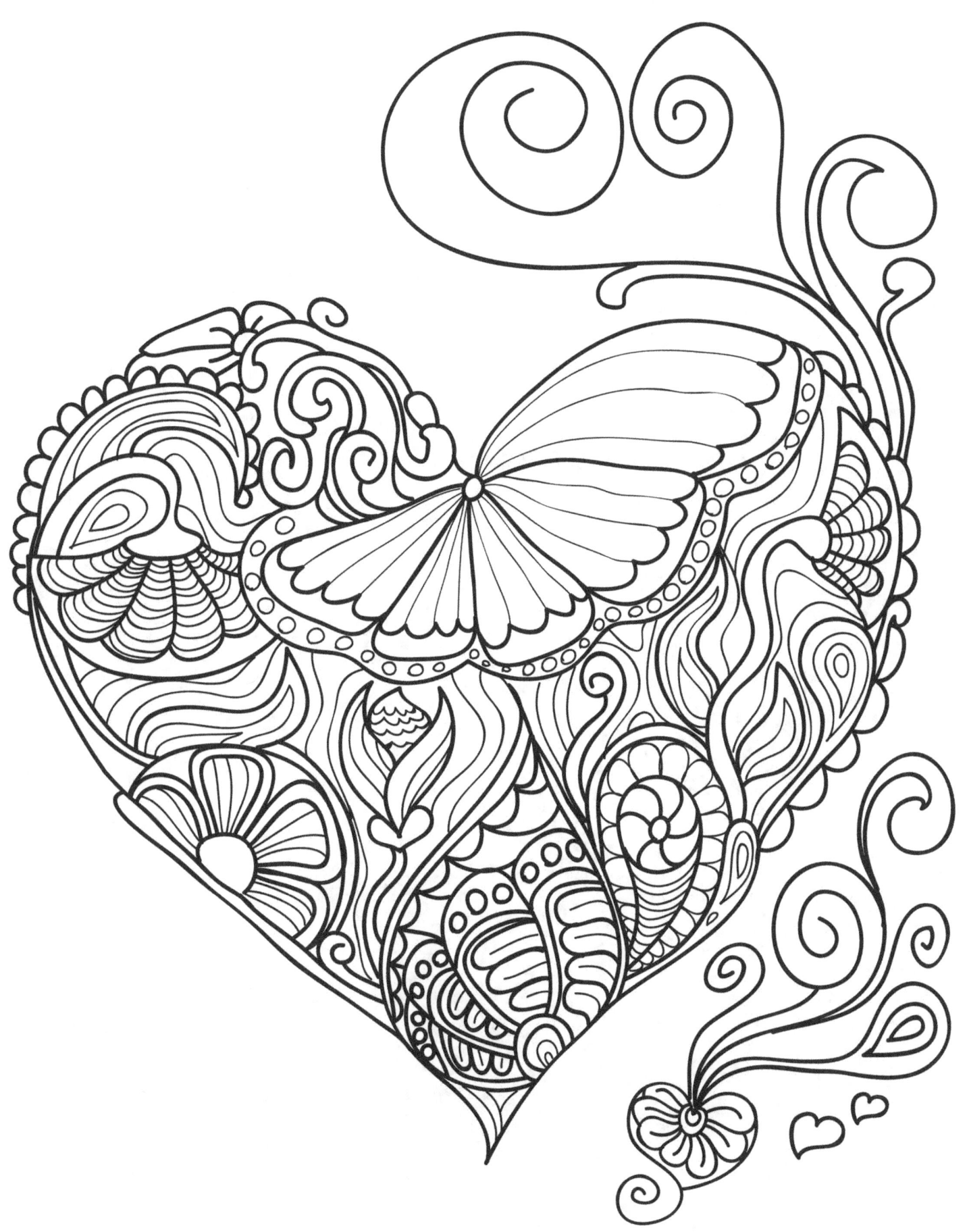

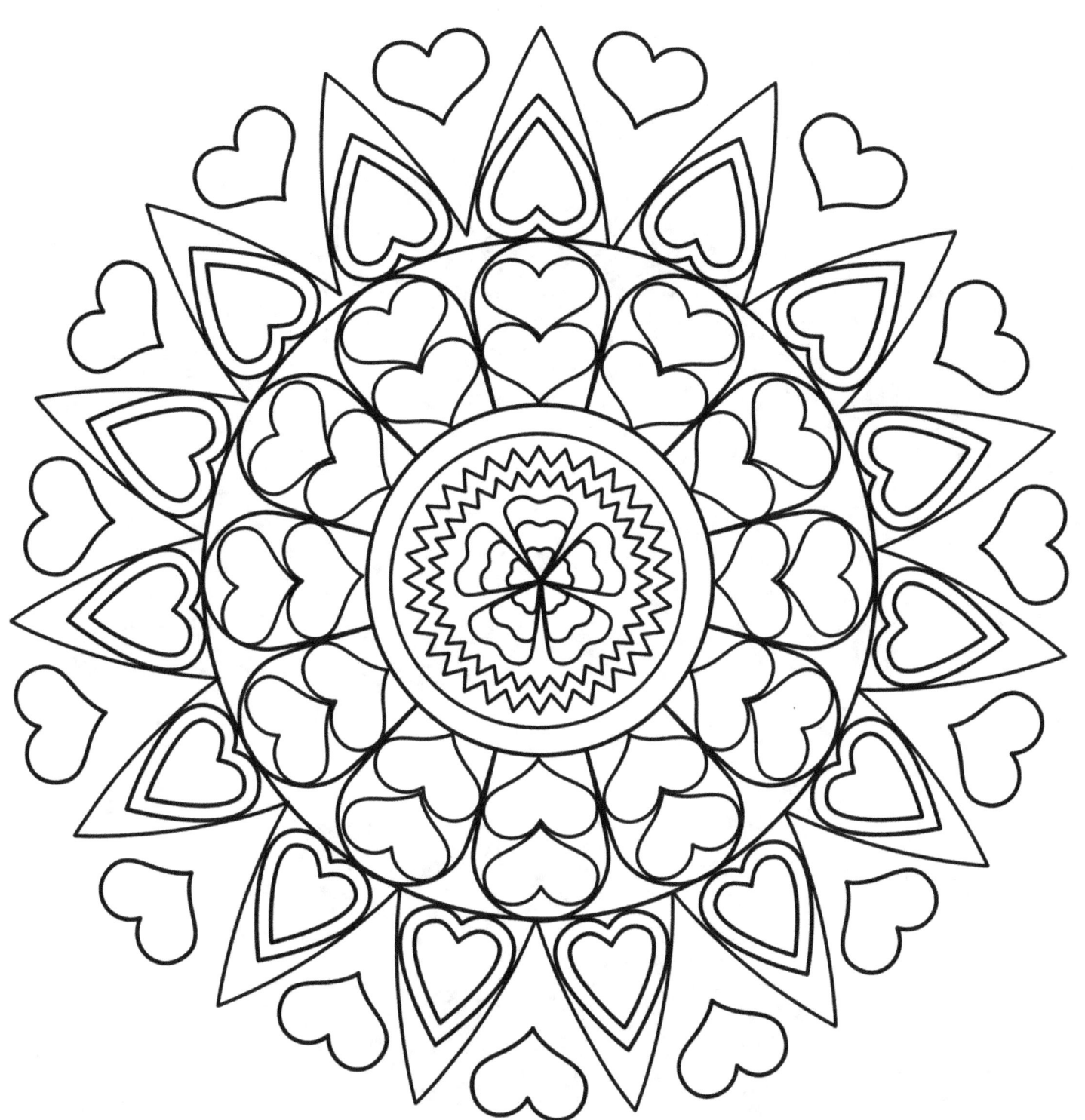

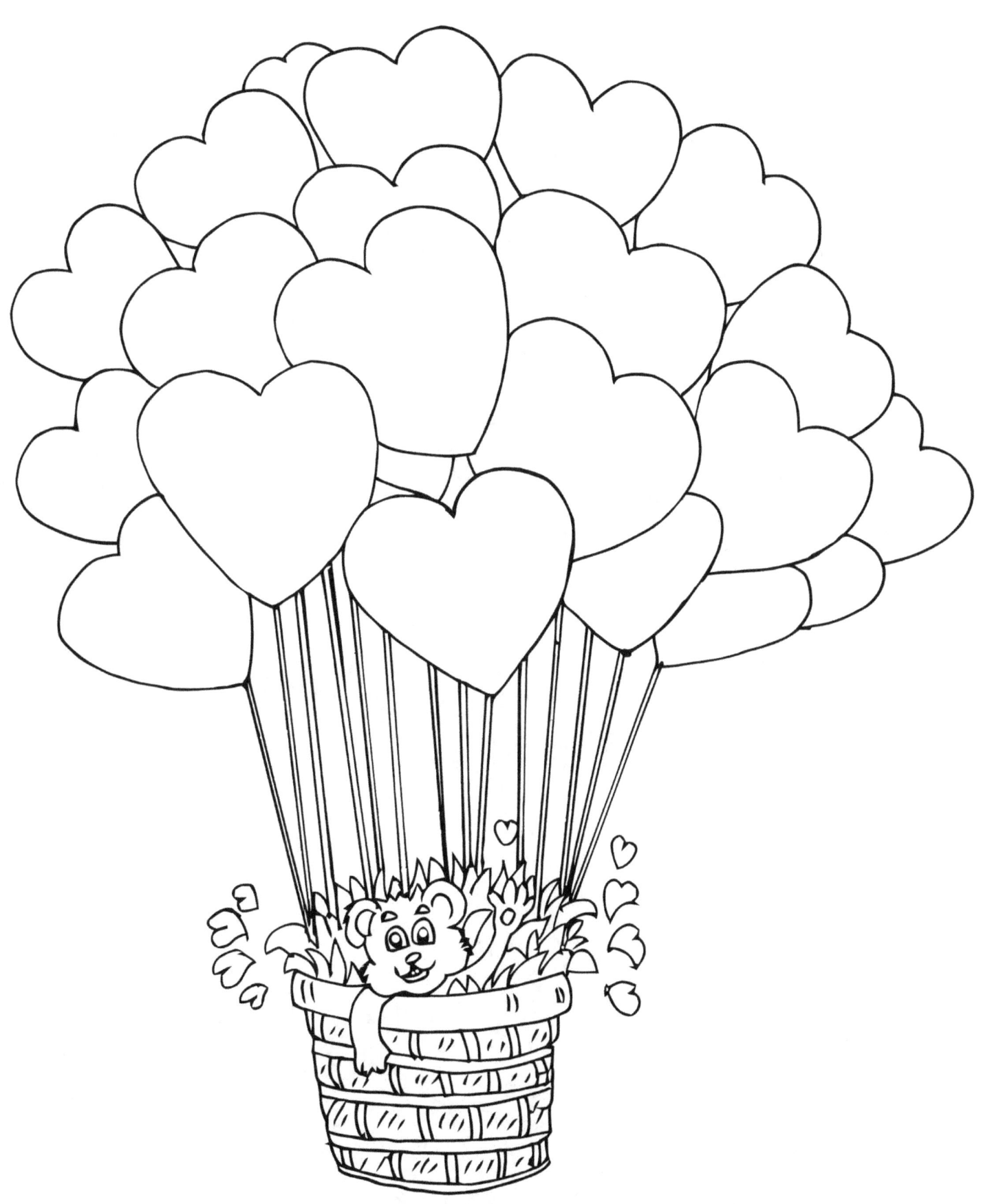

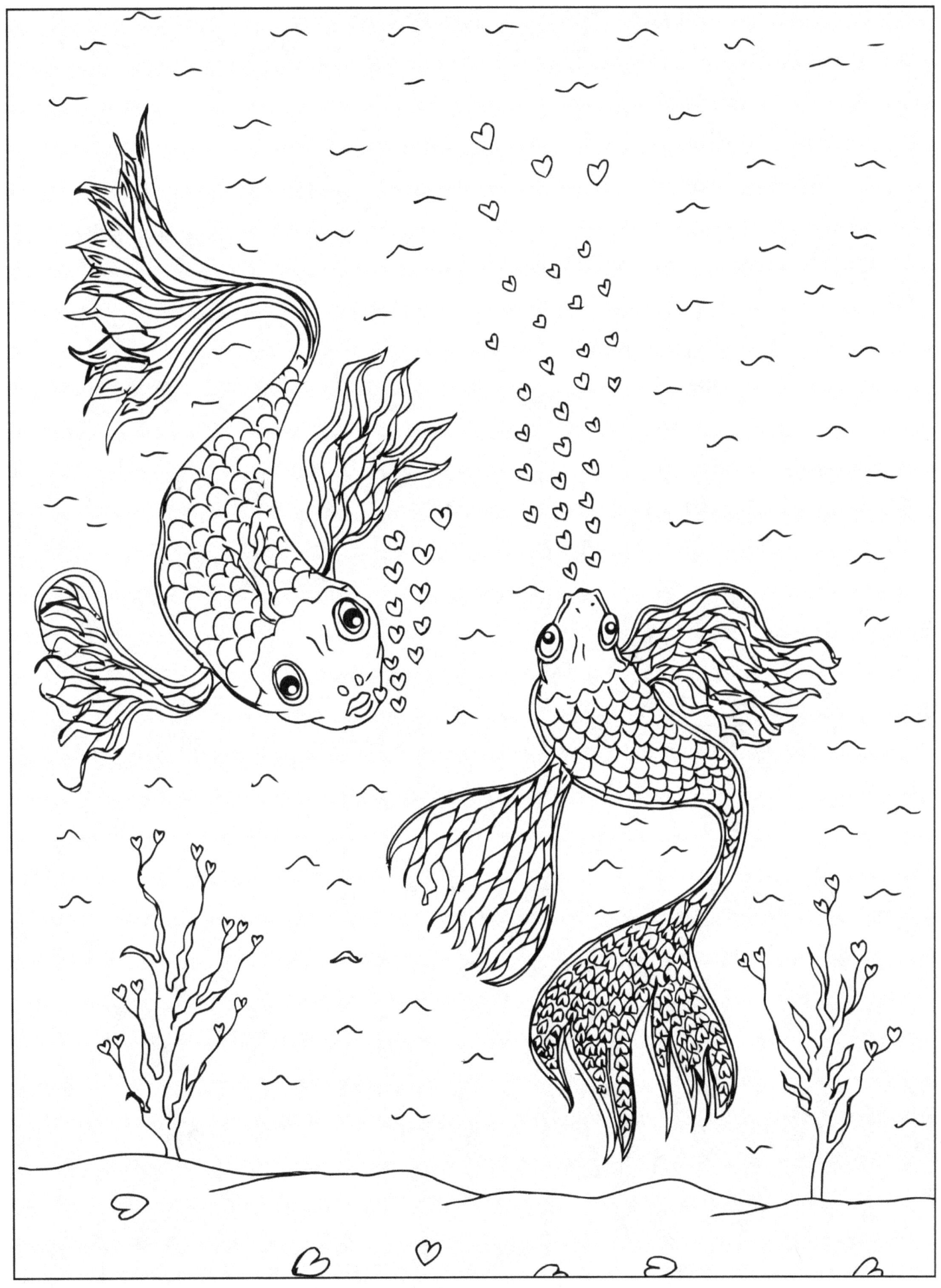

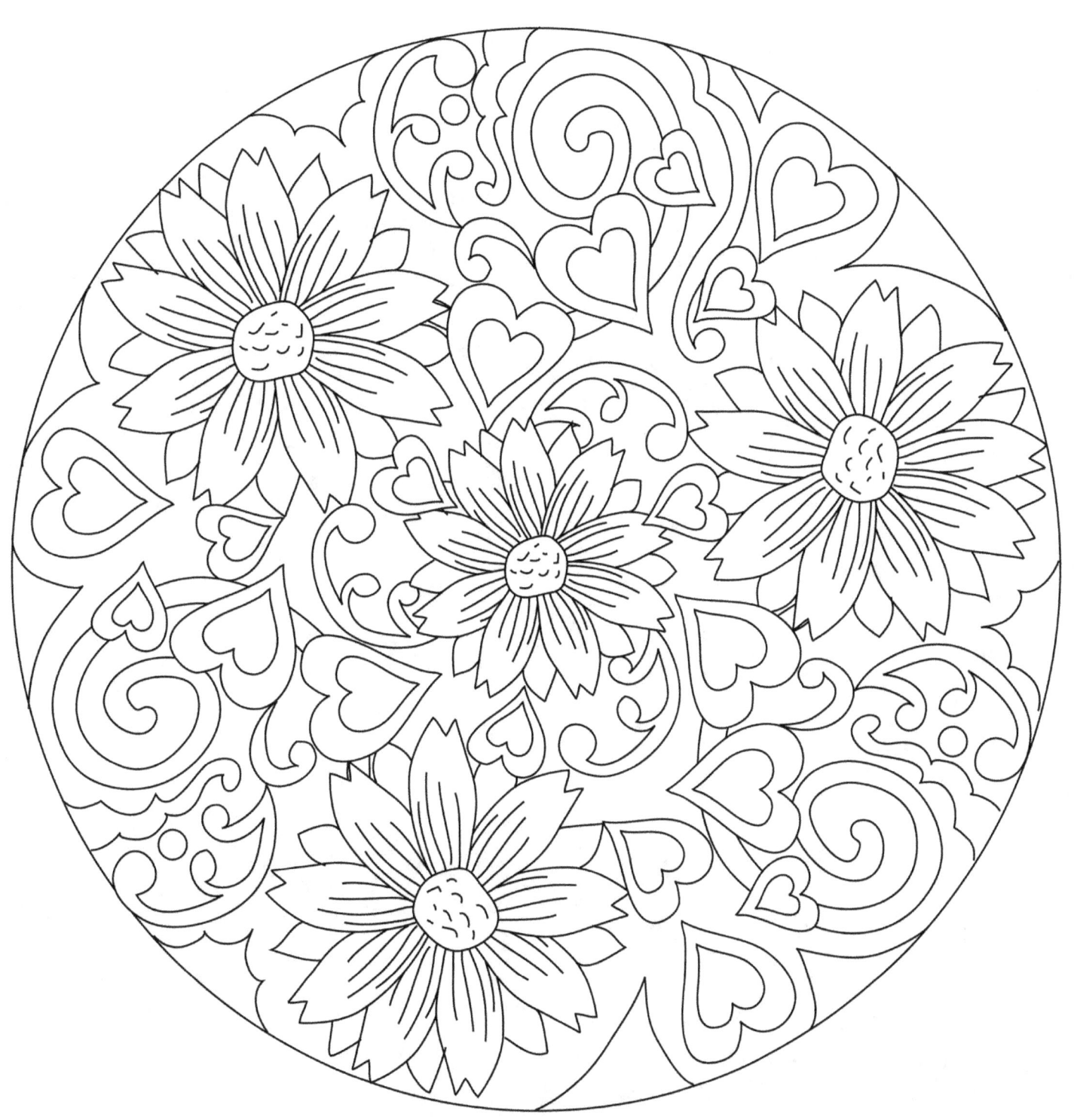

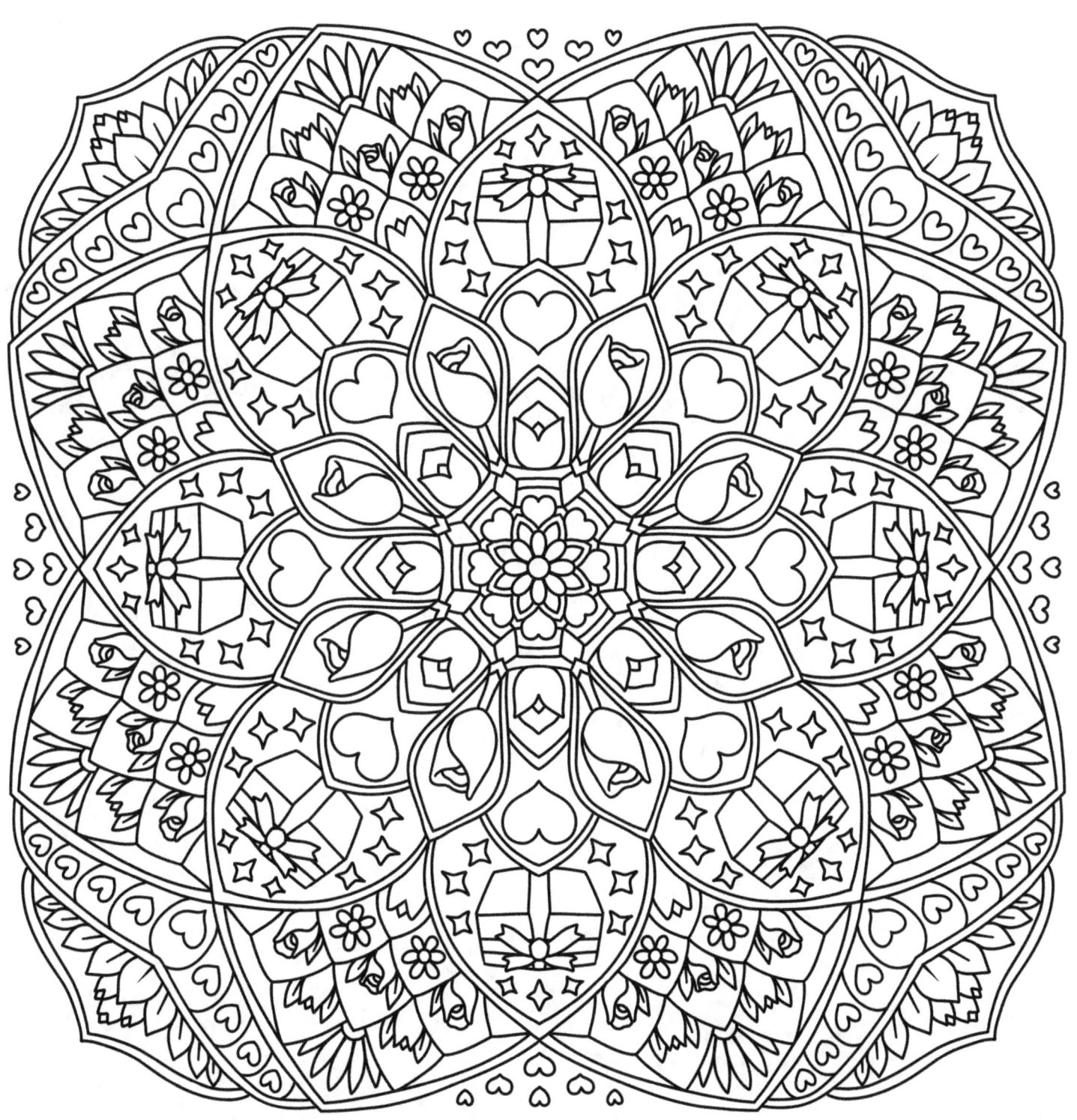

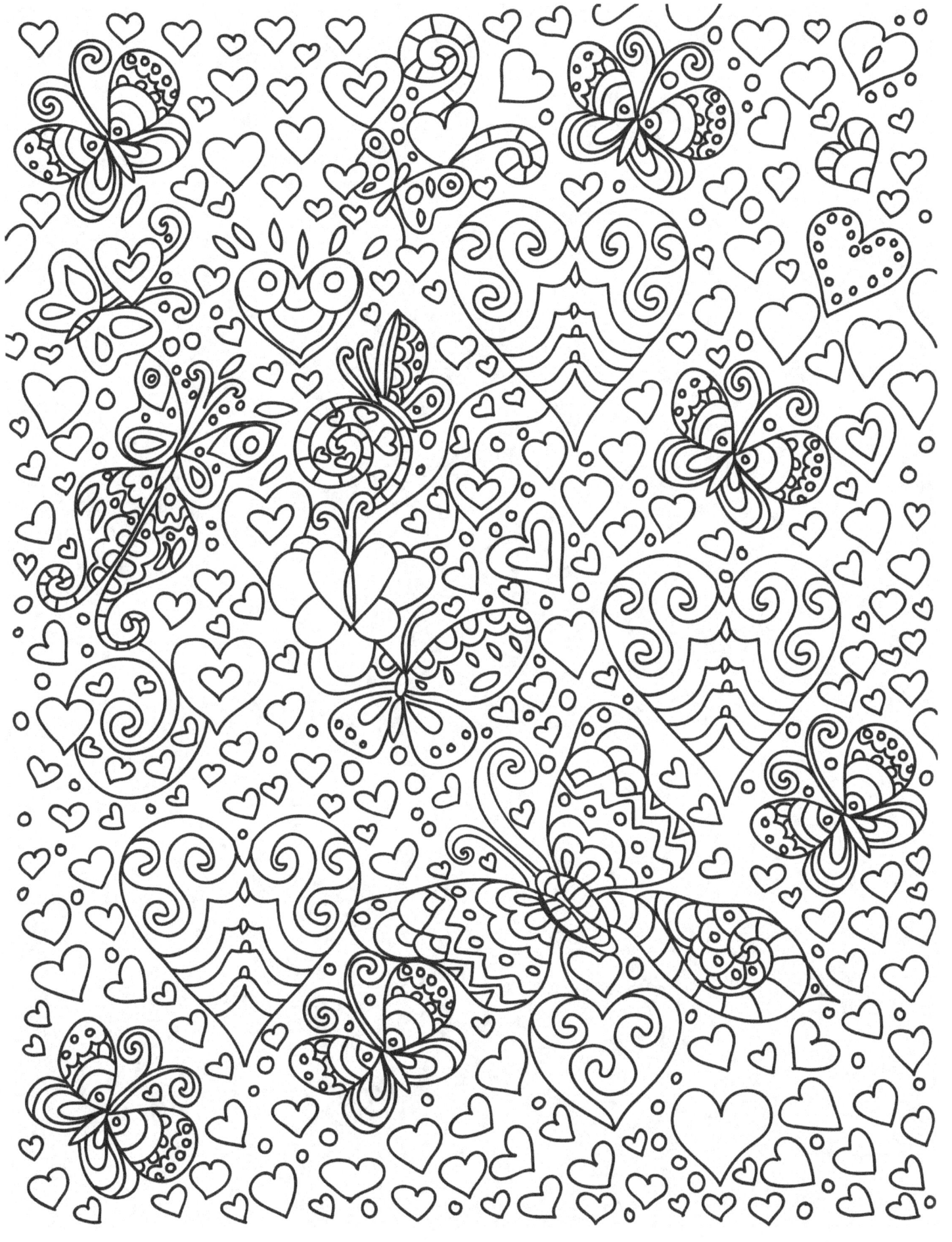

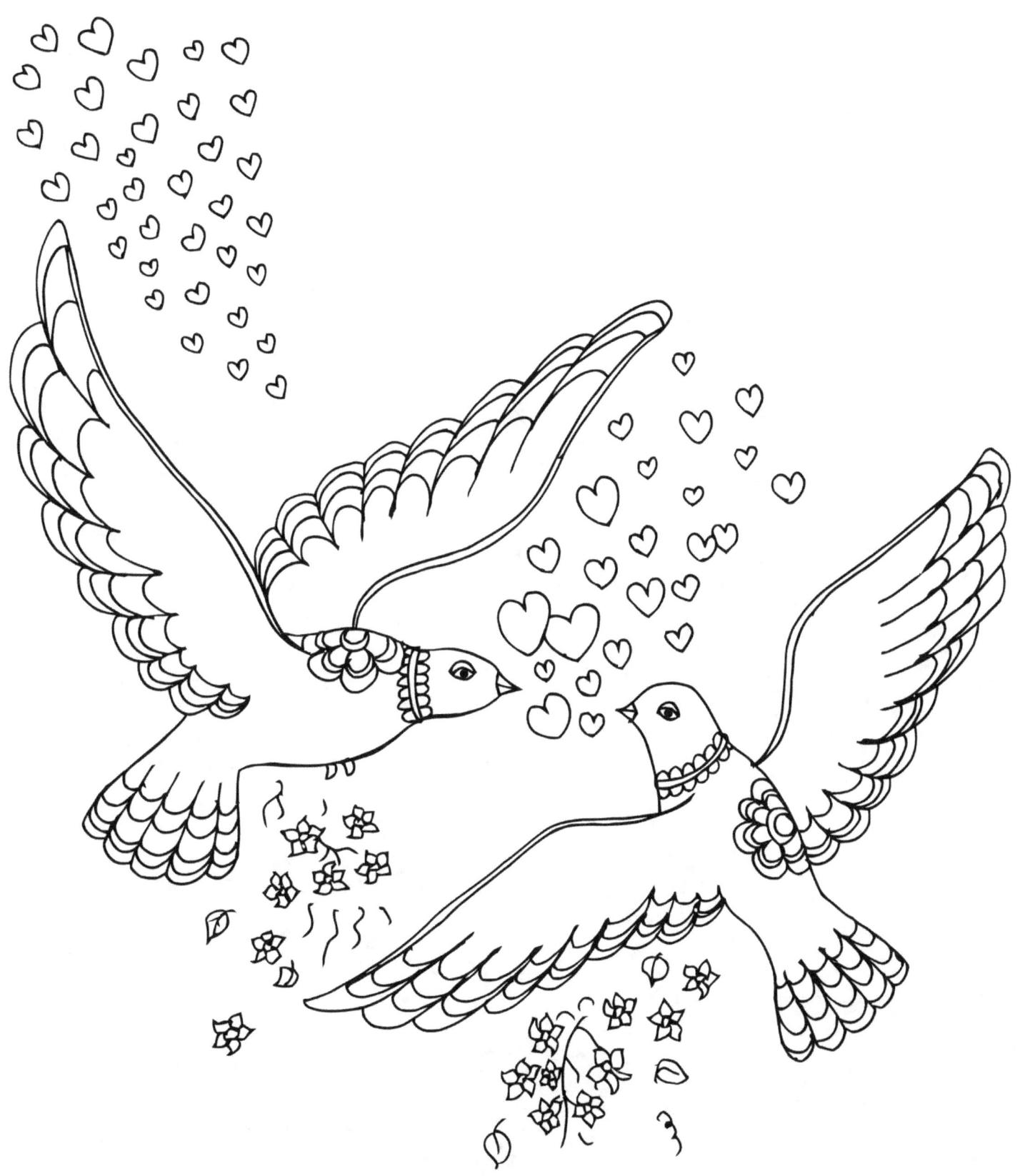

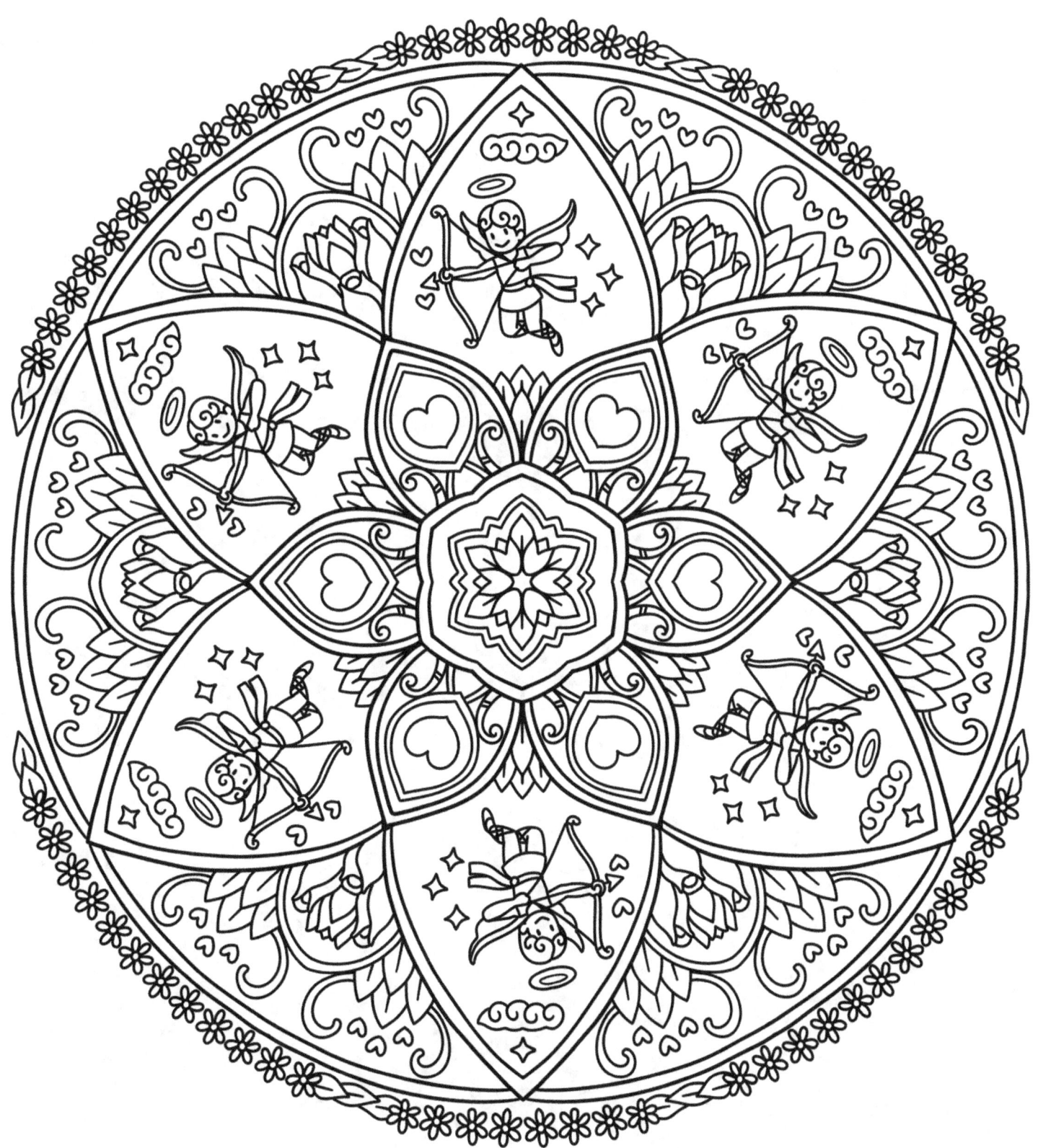

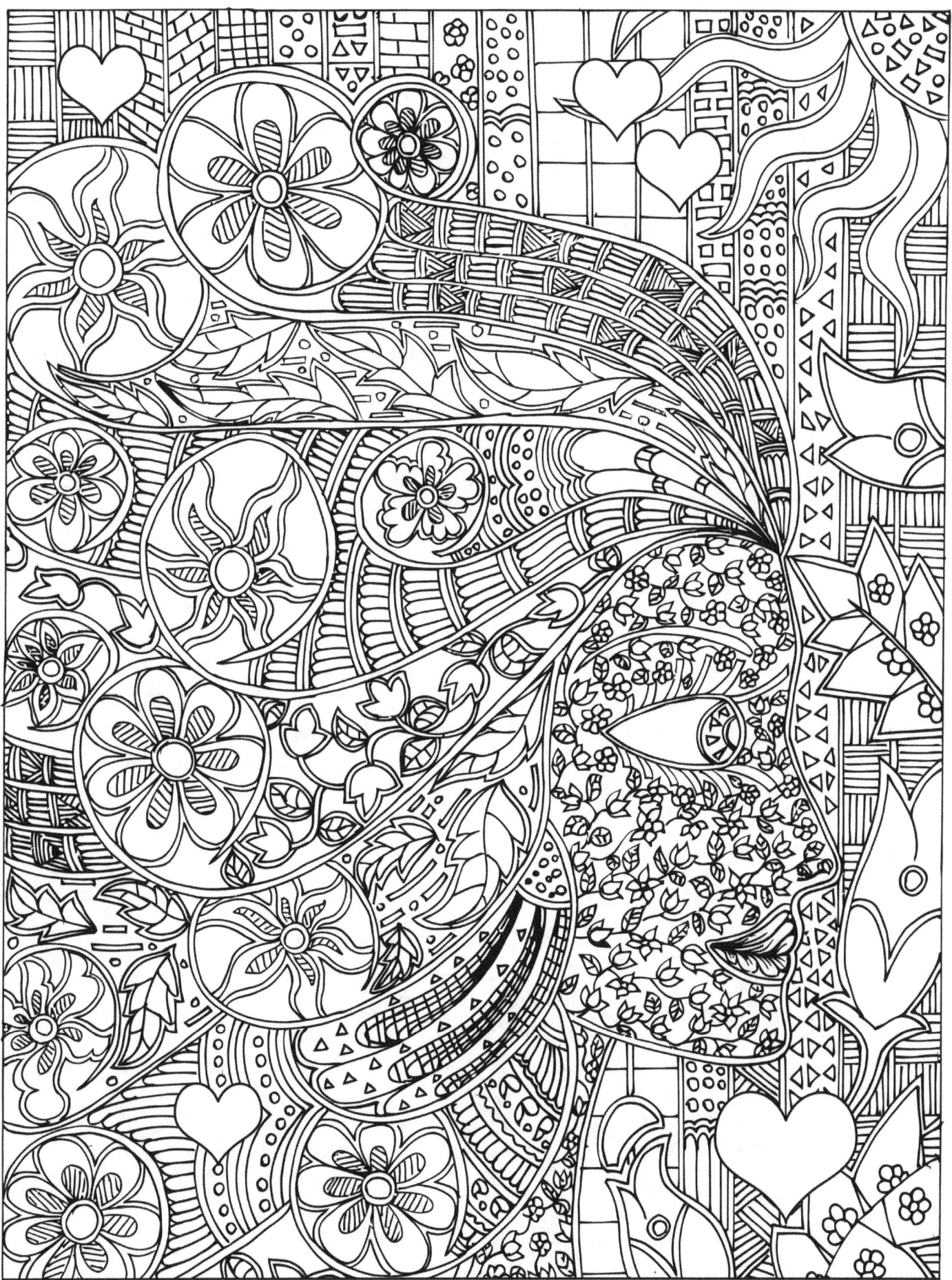

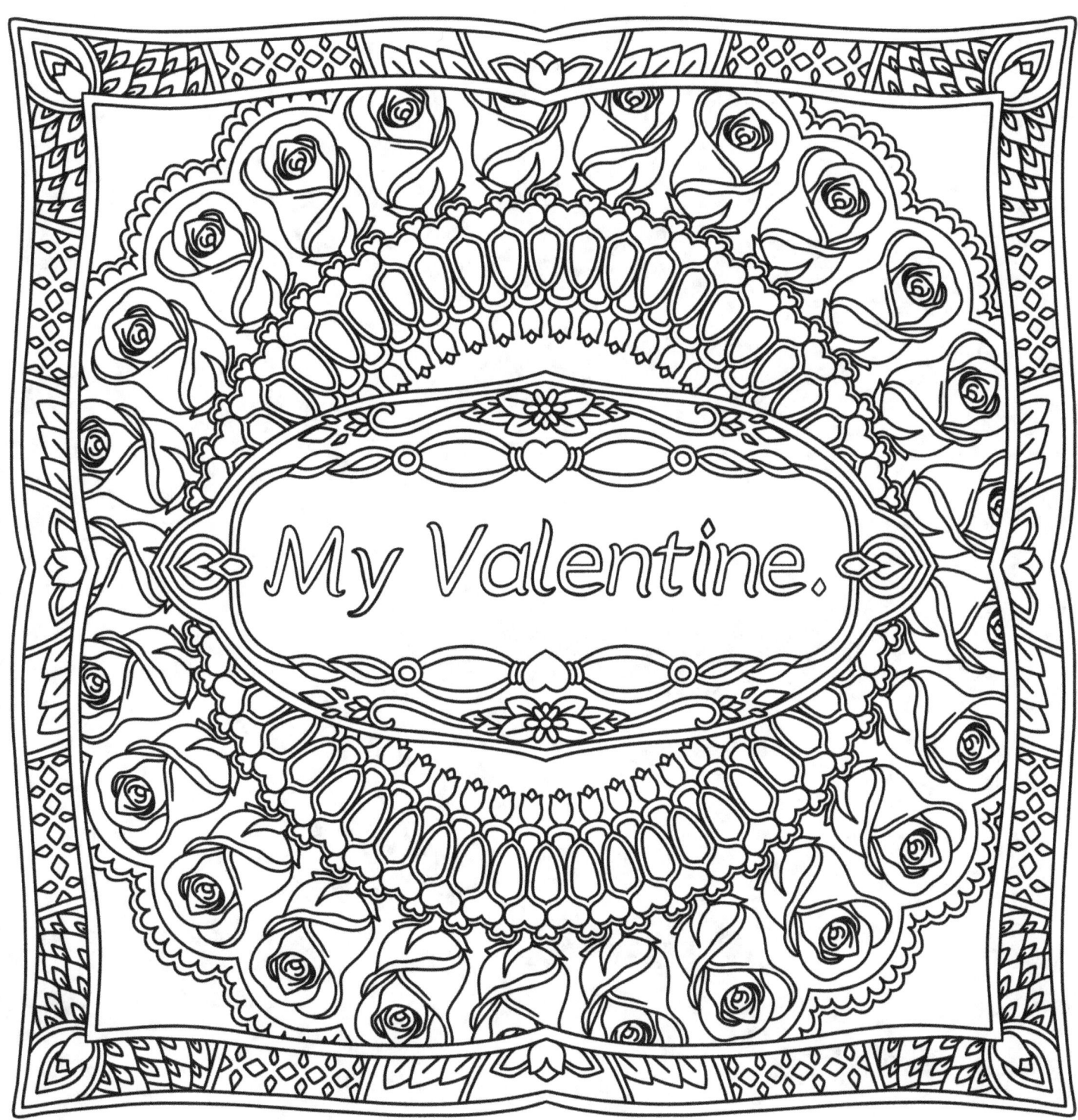

Be one of the In Crowd!

As a Mix Books Coloring Insider, you will receive FREE coloring pages to download and be among the first to know about special offers and our newest coloring books.

Sign up now, and as our thanks to you, immediately receive TEN illustrations in PDF format. Go to:

http://www.mix-booksonline.com/coloring

Other coloring books for you to enjoy:

We Are Gobsmacked: British Sweary: an adult coloring book of British swear words and slang
Christmas Merry and Bright
I Am Woman: A Woman's Coloring Book to Boost Self-Esteem and Nurture Self-Confidence
In an Octopus's Garden: Stress Relieving Patterns
In The Jungle: The Mighty Magical Jungle
Flower Designs: Stress Relieving Patterns
Christmas Mandalas and Messages
Paisley and Patterns: Intricate Designs Coloring Book
Paisley and Patterns Dark Edition
Coloring Book for Adults: BadASS Buttocks
Coloring Book of Vintage Caricatures and Characters
Silesian Folk Tales Coloring Book: Intricate Vintage Illustrations **Coloring Book for Kids:** Farm Animals
Coloring Book for Kids: Monsters
Coloring Book for Kids: Farm Animals
Fun, Fantasy and Fairy Tales: A Kid's Coloring Book
Adult Coloring Book for Relaxation: Serenity
Spirit Guides & Totems
Adult Coloring Book: Stress Relief and Relaxation
Original Hand-drawn Designs
Stress Relief Coloring Book: Patterns & Designs (Adult Coloring Books) www.mixbooksonline.com

Easily access all of our coloring books here:

http://www.mix-booksonline.com/category/coloring-books